In all four Gospels there are men and women whom we have come to know well by name.

But there are others whose part in that story appears almost accidental – they simply happened to be there at the time.

Here Don Cormac tries to identify these unnamed people and to express a little of what they may have felt as they found themselves, unasked and confused, in the greatest story ever recorded. If you were a waiter at the wedding where Jesus turned water into wine, what would your reaction be? How would you feel if you were caught up in the crowd following Jesus to the cross?

Cormac calls these, and many more, the Gospel Bystanders, and his moving tales help to put us in their shoes.

Don Cormac is the pen-name of Angus MacDonald, who was born in London in 1930 and educated at St Peter's School in Woolwich, and Cardinal Vaughan Memorial School in Kensington. After National Service he went up to Trinity College, Cambridge, where he trained as an architect. He worked in private practice then joined the Westminster Bank (now National Westminster Bank), retiring as the bank's Chief Architect in 1990.

A committed Catholic, he was a Foundation Governor of St Wilfrid's RC Secondary School in Crawley and is a regular member of the parish of Worth Abbey. He married Patricia in 1957 and they have four grown-up sons and four grandchildren.

His previous books are *The Road From the Isles* (1992), a history of his family; and *A Place of Safety* (1996), the story of a young boy evacuated from London to Hawkhurst in 1939. He has also written a number of children's stories and his book *The Adventures of Francis the Drake* is a series of stories about a family of Mallard ducks.

WHEN PATHWAYS CROSS

Tales of some
Gospel Bystanders

Don Cormac

The Book Guild Ltd
Sussex, England

First published in Great Britain in 2002 by
The Book Guild Ltd
25 High Street,
Lewes, East Sussex
BN7 2LU

Typesetting in Times by
Keyboard Services, Luton, Bedfordshire

Printed in Great Britain by
Athenaeum Press Ltd, Gateshead

A catalogue record for this book is available from
The British Library

ISBN 1 85776 616 4

To Pat, who first suggested the idea of these stories

CONTENTS

FOREWORD

In all four Gospels, there are men and women whom we have come to know well by name, each of whom figured to a greater or lesser degree in the story of Our Lord's ministry here on earth. There are also others whose part in that story appears to he almost accidental – they simply happened to be there at the time.

Some are identified by something they did. Others we are aware of only by inference. There are one or two who may well have been there but whom we can find only in the imagination. In the Gospel text, none of them has a name.

In these stories, with one exception, all the leading characters are referred to, directly or indirectly, in the Gospels, as the text reference confirms, but their names are my invention. The sole exception is Samuel, but I suggest that the innkeeper could have had a son, and the cemetery would have had a gardener.

I have tried to identify these unnamed people, to put us in their shoes perhaps, and to express a little of what they may have felt as they found themselves, unasked and confused, in the greatest story ever recorded. I call them the Gospel Bystanders.

Don Cormac
July 2001

THE LATECOMERS

'... because there was no room at the inn.'
Luke, ii, 7

Samuel was puzzled. Oh, he knew that at the tender age of seven there was a lot he did not understand, but this was something quite different from anything he had ever seen before, and he was puzzled. Sam lived in a small market town of not many people, most of whom made their living as farmers in the surrounding countryside, or as tradesmen – builders, carpenters and so on – in the town itself. Sam's father and mother ran the local inn. To be truthful, it was really a pub, where the farmers would meet in the evenings to talk over the events of the day and to put the world to rights, but there were some rooms which the family did not need, and so they let them on a 'bed and breakfast' basis which provided the excuse to call the place an inn.

It wasn't a large building, but there were some sheds and barns out at the back, which were usually used as storage, but which recently his father had spent some time clearing up and making tidy, so that, as his father told everybody, they could be brought into use as extra accommodation when the crowds arrived. It was the crowds which were puzzling Sam.

Over the last few days, people had been arriving in the town in droves. They didn't live or work there, but, from what Sam could make out, most of them had been born there and had come back now because they had to put their names down on a list at the Town Hall in the Market Square. Sam couldn't understand why they had to do this, and when he asked his father he was told that it was nothing for him to worry about, but he should be pleased that it was all good for business. Certainly, the bar was always crowded in the evenings, and all the rooms were let, including most of the sheds and barns out at the back.

All this activity had put his father in a very good mood, and Sam was very hopeful of a really good present for his approaching birthday. Very wisely, Sam thought it better to keep quiet then, and not worry his father and mother, who were clearly very busy looking after all these extra customers. All the same, Sam was very, very puzzled, and dying to know what all the fuss was over.

One evening, a few days after this hustle and bustle had begun, Sam went off to bed as usual in his little room up in the roof. He liked his room because from the little window he could see down into the yard behind the hotel, and loved to watch the town as it settled for the night. He was sitting by the window this evening when two strangers, a man and a woman, came to the back door and knocked.

'Now, that's odd,' said Sam to himself. 'Why have they come to the back door?'

Just then his father appeared – Sam drew back from the window lest he be seen, for he should have been in bed – and the unknown man said to him, 'Excuse us coming to the back, but the front was so crowded we couldn't make ourselves heard. My wife and I have just arrived in the town and wondered if you had a room to spare. Everywhere else we have tried is full, and it's so late now that we are getting anxious for somewhere for the night.'

Sam's father did not sound too pleased when he answered, for the customers in the bar needed serving. 'There are no rooms left tonight,' he said. 'Don't you know what's going on in the town? We have been fully booked for days, but I suppose I could let you rough it in one of the barns in the yard. Mind you, it's nothing special, just shelter – and the charge will be the same as for one of the rooms. Take it or leave it, it's up to you.'

The couple had a hurried conversation and agreed to take what was offered. 'It's better than nothing,' said the man to his wife, 'and we'll manage somehow.'

Sam watched as his father led the couple across to the barn, and left them saying, 'You can get something to eat in the inn if you wish, and I can let you have some blankets for the night if you come over with me now, but I must get back.'

The couple thanked Sam's father and said, 'Goodnight, we'll be all right now.'

The barn door closed, and Sam's father went back into the inn, while Sam, tired and now even more puzzled, crept into his bed and went to sleep.

He slept well and deeply, and had a wonderful dream. It was as if the whole sky had been lit up by a huge star, which shone so brightly in the night air, whilst at the same time there was what sounded like a party, with music and singing. It was one of those dreams which seemed to make no sense, and was like nothing Sam had ever experienced before, so that when his mother came in to wake him in the morning he was full of wonder at what he had seen in his sleep.

His mother, however, was far too busy to listen to him for she had been up half the night, and had little sleep herself. 'Oh, I've not got time to listen to you and your dreams,' she said. 'While you have been dreaming the night away that woman who turned up so late last night with her husband – oh of course, that was after you went to bed – well, we had to put them up in the barn, and now, what do you think, she's had a baby – out there in the barn – in the middle of the night! We're all worn out – all except the baby, that is. He's sound asleep – just like a man!' And with that, off she went, leaving Sam feeling a bit fed up that his mother didn't want to hear about his dream.

And he got no attention from his father, either, as he was rushing about the place trying to get ready for the business of the new day. Poor Sam! Nobody seemed to have time for him today and the whole place seemed more crowded than ever. 'But wait a minute,' he said to himself, 'Mum said that a baby was born in the barn last night and he'll not be able to ignore me, so I'll go and see him.' Sam crossed the yard, and went over to the barn. Nervously, he knocked on the door, opened it, and put his head inside to look.

The couple who had come last evening were there, and between them in a makeshift cot lay the little baby boy, sleeping peacefully. Things had happened so quickly last evening that there were some animals still in the barn, but right at the back. The mother and father were being very quiet so as not to disturb the sleeping baby. Sam was very quiet too, for he had never seen such a tiny creature in his whole life. He looked long and hard – and then stole away.

And now, lots of people began coming to the barn to see the baby, and that puzzled Sam. He had thought the couple who came so late were strangers, but the visitors, apart from three rather grand-looking men, were mostly local people, so maybe they were not strangers at all. 'Very odd, then,' thought Sam, 'that they had nowhere to stay last night. But then,' he thought, as a small boy often does, 'grown-ups do some very strange things.'

The activity round the barn continued for several days, until one morning, Sam got up and went to see the little baby as usual, but found to his disappointment and surprise that all three, father, mother, and baby, were gone. The barn was empty, and it was as if nobody had ever been there. Sam went to his father and mother and asked what had happened, but did not get a very satisfactory answer.

'He came in this morning, very early,' said his father, 'and just said they all had to leave at once. Something about they had to get across the border as quickly as possible. I dunno, I reckon there was something fishy about those two, and their baby. At least they paid up in full.'

Sam was sad, for he had enjoyed his visits to see the baby each day, and the couple had always been so nice to him, even letting him hold the little warm bundle once or twice. And they had just gone, without a word. Very, very strange indeed, but, as small boys do, Sam soon found other things to occupy and distract him.

The crowds were less today as the little market town began to resume its peaceful existence, and life was getting back to normal. But the peace did not last long!

Suddenly, the day after the couple and their baby had disappeared in such a mysterious way, the town was woken up noisily with the arrival of a company of soldiers, all armed to the teeth and swaggering round importantly, shouting and swearing. These soldiers belonged to the King, who was cruel and unpopular, and Sam didn't like them at all. Usually, the soldiers did not interfere too much in the affairs of the town, but today was different. Today they were searching all the houses and causing great anger, because without any explanation they were taking away all the little babies they found. Sam just could not understand what was going on. What harm could little babies do to these armed men?

Now they were hammering on the door of the inn, demanding to know if there were any babies there. Sam was too old to interest them – much to the relief of his father and mother – but when his father said that a baby had been born there just three days ago, the soldiers shouted at him and demanded to know where the baby was now. When they were told that he had been taken away by his parents only the day before, the soldiers were furious and wanted to know where they had gone. Sam's father explained that they had simply gone, very early, saying something about 'crossing the border'. At that, the soldiers were even more angry, and set off at a great pace in the direction of the frontier.

With the soldiers gone, things began to get back to normal and the pub was in ferment that morning as people tried to work out what the day's dreadful events were all about. Sam's parents were very busy in the bar, and Sam listened hard to all the chat.

'I just cannot believe it all happened,' said Sam's father to some of the customers. 'What a dreadful thing. All those poor little kids taken like that! There's never been such an upheaval in Bethlehem in all the years I've been here. But I'll tell you this – I knew there was something fishy about that pair. I should never have let them in.'

His wife nodded, sadly, and said, 'Such a lovely little boy they had. There was something special about that child.'

Sam heard what his mother said, and added, 'I liked that baby – they called him Jesus, you know. Do you think we'll ever hear what happened to him?'

A MAN OF SERVICE

'. . . there was a wedding at Cana in Galilee.'
John, ii, 1

Benjamin opened his eyes and peered through the window at the morning. To his relief, the sky was clear with not a cloud in sight, but just a hint of mist which seemed to be the first sign of a beautiful day to come. 'Thank goodness for that,' said Ben, still with the sleep in his eyes. 'What a good day for a wedding!'

He lay for a moment, relishing the warmth of his bed, in that confused early-morning state of reluctant acceptance that there was work to be done. It was his work which had called forth his comment about it being a good day for a wedding. Not that it was his wedding. No, his interest in weddings was simply that he was a waiter at a local inn where, today, there was to be a wedding reception, and for Ben that meant hard work. At least though, he thought, with the weather set fair the guests will be able to stay outside in the gardens, and not get under our feet inside while we are trying to clear away after the wedding breakfast. 'Come on,' he said to himself, 'This won't do at all. Up you get or you'll be late, and then there will be trouble with the boss even before things get going.'

He threw back the bedclothes and got up, stretching and yawning, as he washed and dressed, and got himself ready to go to work. As he snatched a quick breakfast, he found himself, as always at this time of the day, thinking gloomily about the way things had panned out for him. Ben was in his late twenties, and a waiter at the largest inn in the town, not that that was of any great significance in a place the size of Cana. Cana was a small town, hardly more than a large village, in Galilee, and almost unknown to anyone who lived in the big towns and cities further afield. And life in such a town could be extremely dull, following as it did a monotonous, day-to-day pattern. 'Dull and monotonous,' said Ben, 'describes this town and my life exactly.'

It hadn't always been that way, though, for there had been a time when he had been full of ambition, and had dreamed of one day being the head waiter in a large establishment in a big town, even perhaps in Jerusalem. Ah, what price ambition! After his early training in the very hotel where he still worked, he had felt he had the world at his feet, and foresaw a career of progress and advancement well away from this small place where nothing ever happened. Well, it had not happened for him, he thought sadly as he cleared away his breakfast things and set out for work. Disconsolate, he muttered to himself, 'I'm just small fry in a small-fry town.'

As he made his way to the inn, his mind went back over the past ten years or so, trying to work out where and why everything seemed to have gone awry. It was not a difficult exercise. He had always lived with his mother and father in the same house which was still his home. Their only child, he had enjoyed all the benefits and comfort of life at home, and, demanding though his work was, he had always been perfectly at ease nurturing his ambition to better himself in his chosen profession. He enjoyed being of service to his customers, and got great satisfaction from his work. For their part, his parents had always encouraged his ambition, and were always so proud of any advancement or promotion which he gained. The quiet, settled pattern was to change, however, and as the pattern changed so too did Ben – or at least his attitude.

About five years ago, his father, who was foreman in a small bakery, suddenly collapsed and died, leaving Ben's mother distraught. Ben saw it as his duty to stand by his mother now, in spite of the fact that at this very time he had been on the point of taking the plunge and leaving home for the 'big time'. The double blow was bitter, his father dead and an opportunity missed, but he accepted the situation, thinking that this was no more than a slight delay in his plans. As he saw it, this was a hitch, no more than that, and his ambition was undiminished. A year or two, he thought, and all would be back on course.

A year went by, and Ben was concerned to see that his mother showed little sign of getting over his father's death. In fact, if anything, her condition was deteriorating. Her decline went on, gathering pace, until soon she was in need of almost constant care and attention, all of which Ben gave willingly to a mother who meant so much to him. Meanwhile, he continued to give good service in the inn, and was well-thought of there, gaining some advancement from time to time. In fact, he was even led to believe by the owner that he could perhaps be considered for the position of head waiter, when the present incumbent retired in a year or two. That, to Ben, was an encouraging sign, not just because the hints that were given, but because they indicated that he was capable of higher things, that his ambition was not ill-founded.

He still had in mind, one day, to leave Cana and make his fortune elsewhere, but that could not be yet, he realised. Fate now took a further hand, and Ben's life was again thrown into turmoil when his mother, weak and broken-hearted, fell ill and, after a short time, died. Ben was shattered. The loss of both parents in such a short time was almost too much. The adjustment to his new life on his own was hard indeed, but his work was his saviour, with, as he thought, a reasonable prospect for the future. But now came the final blow, when the head waiter retired early – and was replaced by a younger man from another town who was known to the family of the owner. So much for half-given promises. Ben's disappointment was total.

He felt let down, unwanted and totally alone. Almost overnight, all his ambition was gone. What hope had he now, having, through no fault of his own, put back his plans, twice, and then been denied a post he had been given to think might have been his own. His grand plans were in tatters, and even here in Cana there seemed to be little future for him. Thoroughly confused and disillusioned, he had decided to stay in Cana where at least he had work he enjoyed, albeit under a new boss. He was not prepared to risk further setback by stepping into the unknown. As Ben reported for work that bright and sunny morning, he was not a happy man, but, as so often in the recent past, his work would come to his rescue. At least it would take his mind off his disappointment.

Ben was now twenty-eight years old, and all those unhappy things had happened two years ago. He had fallen into a regular way of life now, both at work and at home, and had all but forgotten those grand plans he had once entertained. He had persuaded himself that Cana would have to do. So now to today, he thought. It was certainly going to be busy, for the wedding was a big affair and the guests many and important. There was no room today for error, he told himself, and went to work with a will to succeed.

There was much to be done long before any guests arrived. Tables to be set out and properly laid, extra chairs to be moved in, flowers to be arranged, buffets to be laid out, the wine, delivered only last evening by the groom, to be brought up ready for serving. Oh, a thousand things to be remembered, but, then, all this activity occupied the mind as well as the body. Ben's concentration was total, and needed to be, as the new head waiter had more than once mentioned that some of the guests were friends of his and that there could be no slip-up in service today – or else!

Bride and groom arrived, with their families and friends, and very soon Ben and his colleagues were run off their feet admininstering to their every need, and answering calls from all round the room. 'Waiter, over here!' 'Waiter, please!' Come here, go there, do this, do that. There was no respite at all, as the party went with a swing, conversation – and wine – flowing with abandon. Everything was going so well as to induce complacency – but suddenly that complacency was shattered. And completely!

Ben had seen the groom speaking quietly to the head waiter, and was concerned when he was summoned to join them.

'Ben,' said the head waiter, 'we have trouble! We're out of wine.'

'Out of wine,' said Ben, 'how can that be? All that was ordered came in last night. What's happened?'

'There wasn't enough. That's what,' was the reply. 'So now what are we going to do?'

The groom, meanwhile, had been talking to one of the guests he knew, a lady from nearby Nazareth, who had come with her son and some of his friends. The lady now was speaking to her son, her face showing concern.

Ben did not hear what she said, but did overhear the son's reply, which was strange in the extreme.

'But you know, mother, that my time has not yet come.'

What on earth could he mean, thought Ben, but before he could think anything more of it, the son had got up and spoken to the head waiter, who was now coming across to Ben and the other waiters.

'Don't ask me any questions,' said the head waiter, 'but just do what this young man tells you. His mother thinks he may be able to get us out of this mess.'

The son, who was about the same age as Ben, perhaps a little older, came over and, speaking quietly, said to the assembled staff, 'Would you please fill those large jars with water,' indicating a row of big stone vessels, 'and then leave me for a moment of silence.' His face had a look of total serenity, but of confidence too, even of power, as he spoke, and without any query the waiters did as he asked. The water pots filled, they fell back, watching the young man as he stood in silent concentration. A moment passed, and he spoke again, this time to the head waiter. 'Would you please taste?' he said, pointing to the jars. The head waiter did as asked, and tasted.

Amazement spread across his face. 'But this is the finest wine, and how can that be? There was only water, and now...' His voice tailed off in a mixture of wonder, admiration – and perhaps some fear. He recovered himself enough to turn and berate his staff to be about their duties and serve this wondrous new wine, and the staff in their turn were perplexed at what they had seen.

The young man had returned to his mother's side, and she smiled her gratitude. It was as if she had known that something quite unusual was going to happen. The banquet proceeded, served by some very puzzled waiters, very puzzled indeed. And none more so than Ben, who had witnessed the whole thing from close quarters. That young man had had a profound effect on Ben. He had seen a man of his own age, displaying great concentration – almost as if he were in deep prayer – do the most incredible thing that Ben could have conceived. That water had been changed into wine, and not just any old wine, but first-class wine. In so doing he had saved the wedding from calamity. He had changed disaster to success. Ben thought again of that man's face as he had wrought such wonder. Never had he seen such strength, such peace, such power in a human face. There was only one word Ben could think of which summed up all he had seen in that face. It was faith! Faith that all was not lost, that there was a solution to the problem, and Ben realised at that moment that the man's moment of concentration had indeed been prayer.

Ben somehow managed to complete all his work that day, but before he went home, he asked the head waiter who the young man was, and where he came from.

'Oh, he comes from Nazareth where his father is a carpenter. I believe his name is Jesus, but I'm not sure.'

'Well,' said Ben, 'I have a feeling that before very long we will all know a lot more about him. I have never come across such a man in all my life. You mark my words, he is something special. He is a man of real service!'

Back in the quiet of his own home, Ben thought about the day, and the incredible thing he had witnessed. No-one would ever believe his story, but of course there were a whole lot of others who had been there as well who could corroborate what he said. But there was more. As far as Ben was concerned, much more. He had been shown today that all was not lost, even in the face of great difficulty. That man, Jesus, a man of about his own age, had shown what faith, yes and prayer, could do to change the impossible to the possible.

So thought Ben, what am I about in Cana, buried in disappointment and disillusionment? He has shown me that anything can be made better, but I must help myself if my life is to be worthwhile. And from that day, Ben's resolve and ambition was rekindled. That day, he had been shown the power of faith.

FISHING WITH MY FATHER

'*...five barley loaves and two fish.*' John, vi, 9

It was well into the evening when David and his father, Onias, arrived home, and just late enough for his mother, Rachel, to be feeling a little apprehensive, since she had expected them back before dusk. Her welcome betrayed her anxiety, but if she was brusque in her manner, it was from genuine concern, not anger.

'Where on earth have you two been till this time?' she demanded of them. 'I've had your supper ready for ages. Come on, David, a quick wash, then eat your supper and off to bed.' And to his father, 'What are you thinking of, keeping the boy out till this time?'

David was trying to speak, his face flushed with excitement, but all he managed to say was, 'Mum, you'll never guess what has happened today. You see, we—' His mother interrupted his outburst, and hushed him, sharply. 'David! Wash, eat and bed, and you can tell me all about whatever it is tomorrow.'

'But, Mum,' said David. Again his mother hushed him with a look that spoke volumes, so David, wisely, did as he was told, and went off to wash before supper.

'What has been going on?' demanded Rachel of her husband when the boy had gone out of the room. His reply was strange in the extreme for a man she knew as quiet and reserved.

'We have had the day to surpass all days, and it's given me all the excitement I'll need for the rest of my life,' he said.

At that moment David burst back into the room saying, 'Dad, have you told Mum about that man, and all those people, and what we saw?' he asked, 'and have you told her about—' His mother broke in quickly. 'David! Supper! Now!'

David sat down and made an attempt to eat, but after a mouthful or two he put down his spoon. 'I'm not really hungry, Mum. I've had plenty to eat while I was out with Dad, because, you see, we—'

'If you're not hungry, David, then bed, so off you go,' said his mother.

'But, Mum, I want to tell you about today.'

'Not tonight, David. You can tell me all about it tomorrow – if you've not forgotten it all by then. Come on, now. Say "Goodnight" to your father, and off you go.'

David made one last try. 'Dad, can't I stay up just a bit tonight – please?'

But Onias, torn between his son's plea and loyalty to his wife, said 'No, David, your mother's right. It'll keep till the morning, and you can tell her then. Sleep well, son, for it's been quite a day. Quite a day, indeed!'

David went, reluctantly, to bed, a very tired little boy, for he was only nine, and was soon fast asleep.

Downstairs, Rachel said to her husband, 'What has got into that boy? He's tired out, but not hungry, and I've rarely seen him so worked up. Just what have you two been up to today? Eh?'

'Sit down, Rachel,' said Onias. 'I'm going to tell you something you will find hard to believe. In fact, I'm not sure I'd believe it if I hadn't been there to see it.' And he began to tell her about their day.

David and his parents lived on their small farm just on

the outskirts of Bethsaida, a town near the Sea of Galilee. The farm kept them self-sufficient, and they supplemented their income by selling their vegetables and eggs in the weekly market in the town. The farm did not allow much leisure time for Onias and Rachel, but today was going to be special, for today David was going fishing with his father. David had been looking forward to this day for ages, and especially to the thought of catching his own fish. His Dad had said, too, that they would light a fire by the waterside and grill their catch to eat for their midday meal. So as well as the fishing gear, they had packed some of his mother's freshly-baked bread in the wicker basket from the shed.

They set off bright and early with his mother's admonition 'Don't be too late home,' ringing in their ears. 'Look at them,' she said to herself as they went off. 'They're like two kids together,' but she took great pleasure in the sight of father and son enjoying the prospect of a day out together.

It took them about half an hour to get down to the lake, and they made for a particular little cove Onias knew, with a secluded beach and which enjoyed the shade of some cedar trees where they could eat in the cool – if, that is, they caught anything. The cove was just out of sight of the road which led from the farm into town about three miles away. David's father had always found the fishing in this cove quite good, for the fish seemed to like the shade and the cool water, and just as importantly on one side of the cove some rocks jutted out into the water which provided a natural jetty from which to cast.

David was in his element, enjoying both his father's undivided attention and the thrill of the fishing. He thought it was just great, especially when by mid-morning they had caught two large fish, not to mention plenty of smaller ones, which his father insisted on putting back in the water.

'If we put them back small,' he said, 'they will grow bigger and make a decent meal for somebody when they're caught again.'

The sun was high and the day getting hot now, so, leaving their nets for a while, they found some driftwood on the beach and built a fire over which they grilled the two big fish to preserve them from the heat of the day. Once cooked and cooled, the fish were carefully wrapped in a cloth and put into the basket under the trees, to be eaten later in the day.

They had gone back to the fishing, when, sometime much later in the morning, they heard some sort of commotion out on the road. There were many voices, and the sound of people on the move. Curious as small boys are, David had to go and have a look, and was astounded to see a crowd, a huge crowd, all milling about on the land across the road. There were hundreds and hundreds of them. 'Hey, Dad, look at this,' he called out excitedly to his father. 'Look at all these people. What are they doing here? Where have they all come from?' He had never seen so many people in one place before.

His father came up the bank and looked, and he too was astounded. It looked as though the whole population of Bethsaida was out here, and he was as curious as his little son to know what was going on. 'Let's get our gear together, David, and go over and investigate. We can come back and fish again, later.'

So they collected up all their gear, and the basket under the trees, and joined the crowd. It was mostly men, some women, but very few youngsters like David. David, being small, pushed his way through the crowd, up to the front, to see what was going on, his father with him.

The crowd was being addressed by a bearded man who

spoke clearly, without shouting, in a gentle yet firm voice. There was no trace of harangue in that voice, but rather a tone of convincing persuasion. He spoke of concern for oneself and also for others, of compassion, and often returned to his central theme of 'all men are brothers'. He spoke fluently and at length, and although much of what he said was above David's head, even as a small boy he found something magnetic in this man who could attract so many to listen to him. To David's father, the words were something the like of which he had never in his life heard. Father and son, each in his own way, were captivated by what this man was saying, and it was with some regret that they realised that they had missed the first part of the address while they were fishing.

Onias said to the man next to him 'Who is this man who speaks in such a way?'

'Oh,' came the reply, 'he's that preacher called Jesus, from Nazareth, who's been causing such a stir all over the place. Some even say he is a new prophet. He certainly has some strange views about living. Interesting, though. Maybe there's something in what he says. I dunno.'

There seemed now to be an earnest conversation going on between the speaker and some of his associates, and word filtered down to the front of the crowd that the discussion was all about how to feed all these people. It seemed they had no money, and even if they had there was nowhere nearby to buy food anyway.

Now enquiry was being made among the crowd as to whether anyone had brought any food with them, and it was soon clear that few, if any, had thought of that. David's father let slip that David had some bread and fish in his basket, and at once one of the speaker's friends asked David just what he had. David told him, haltingly, that he had two fish and five small loaves.

The man laughed and said to the man, Jesus, 'But what is that among so many?'

'No matter,' said Jesus, 'let me have them, please, and get everybody to sit down on the grass.'

Now David was alarmed. He was very proud of the fish he had, the very first he had ever caught, and was loath to let them go – and to someone he had never set eyes on until an hour before. He clutched his basket and looked at his father for support, suddenly feeling much smaller even than his nine years.

To his surprise, his father said, 'It's all right, David, let them have the basket.'

David handed it over, it must be said, very grudgingly. He didn't want to lose those fish. They were his, and he had been looking forward so much to eating his catch.

His father squeezed his hand reassuringly, and whispered, 'Don't worry David. We can always catch more another day. You'll see.' But David was not convinced, as the basket was taken from his grasp.

What happened next defied belief. The man, Jesus, held the basket, stood in silent meditation over it for a moment and then said to his friends, 'Share the food among the people.'

Those nearby said to one another 'What food? There's only two fish and five little loaves. What can he mean?'

They were about to find out, for to the amazement and bewilderment of everyone there the two fish and five loaves contrived to provide the whole crowd with as much as they could eat – and there was plenty left over! It filled twelve baskets, no less!

David and his father were thunderstruck, first by what they had heard, and now by witnessing the impossible. They could understand the words 'Help your neighbour', but this was beyond their comprehension. And they had really seen it happen! The sheer wonder of it all made

David forget the disappointment at losing the precious fish. In fact, he was now feeling quite proud that 'his' fish had helped to save the day. His father, however, knew in his heart that this was something more than just feeding a crowd. It was this man, Jesus, who had made it happen as if to confirm and illustrate his words about sharing and about neighbourliness. This man was someone very special indeed.

The crowd, now fed, dispersed slowly, agog over the events of the afternoon, and David and his father began to make their way home. It took them some time, mixed up as they were with about five thousand people, and it was just after dusk when they arrived at the farm to be greeted by a worried wife and mother.

Onias drew breath and looked at his disbelieving, bemused wife. 'That, my dear, is what happened today. That is why we were late home. Now you can understand why David is so worked up. He has seen something wonderful today.'

Rachel was looking at him as if he were crazy, as if he were a stranger, for her sensible, quiet husband would never talk such nonsense, she was telling herself. He was so earnest about the whole thing.

Again, he said to her 'That is what happened, and David will tell you exactly the same in the morning. He won't forget today – ever – and neither will I. Don't ask me to explain the how or the why of today, but I'll tell you this. That man, Jesus, is no ordinary preacher. He said and did things today that will change the world – and all with such intense feeling for others. He's certainly given me a lot to think about!'

A BURDEN EASED

'... he went to a town called Nain.'
Luke, vii,11

It was pretty late when I got home last night, long after my parents because I had had good reason to stay longer at the reception. The house was quiet when I let myself in and went up to bed. I was dog-tired, exhausted in fact, both physically and mentally. What a day it had been! I think I had experienced every human emotion in a very short time, and once back in the peace of my own home the impact of the day really hit me. It must have been, partly anyway, the sheer relief that the whole thing was over, for I had been dreading that day's dawning. My emotions were drained and I had no strength left, for I had just come home from the funeral of my oldest friend.

The death of any friend is sad and the feeling of loss great, but when you have known someone for as long as I had known Joel that feeling is overpowering. Joel and I had known one another for almost as long as we had both lived, for our mothers had been friends before us, so that when we were born it was almost as if we were related. We were not, of course, but as one had taken his first step, spoken his first words, had his first tumble, then so had the other. We could not have been closer, and, perhaps even more surprisingly, our friendship had strengthened as time went by. Then Joel died, suddenly, and, adding to my grief, his mother had asked me to be one of the pall-bearers at his funeral. Can you see now, why the day had been such a trial for me, why I was in so desolate a frame of mind, and why I felt exhausted?

I had been terrified of the responsibility of agreeing to her request, but could not refuse this last service to my old friend, and hoped that I would gain the strength from somewhere to see me through. The other three bearers were cousins of Joel's of some sort, and I knew them but vaguely, but we all shared the past friendship of a good man, young though he was. He was only twenty-two when he had become ill and died very suddenly, leaving his widowed mother distraught and alone. It was not a moment to shirk reponsibility, I realised, and with much misgiving, went off yesterday morning to say farewell to my boyhood friend. It was in weariness and relief that I undressed and went to bed.

Tired though I was, sleep would not come easily last night. My body needed rest, but my brain refused to give in and so I lay, trying to come to terms with the events of the day, my mind so full of memories. Joel and I had gloried in discovering things together, and as small boys we, more often than not, discovered things of which our parents did not approve. As a result, we both soon realised that our escapades could bring punishment of one sort or another, so that half the fun was making sure we were not caught. I smiled as I remembered the time we had been caught red-handed in his mother's larder spreading her newly-baked bread with the honey his father had just brought in. We denied it, of course, not realising that the sticky mess all round our mouths rather gave the game away. I think we were about four years old!

I was drifting in and out of sleep by now, in that strange in-between world of dream and reality where it is so easy to become confused as to what is fact and what is not. There was that calamitous day when we were both, we thought, trying to be helpful for once and attempting to put away all my mother's best crockery in the cupboard. Good intention overcame capability however, and between us we dropped the whole lot, to see most of it smashed into fragments on the kitchen floor. Much to our surprise – and relief – this mishap had not attracted the awful punishment we had expected, because my mother, while not best pleased, had recognised that for once in our little lives we had actually been trying to help. I think that was probably the day we found out that even grown-ups sometimes could show good sense!

Later, there were wonderful times when we had been allowed to go off together, with some food in our bags, fishing, or, as we regarded it, on an expedition of discovery to some foreign land to fight dragons or whatever you fought in distant parts. The fishing explanation usually served us well when we returned with torn or soaking wet clothes, or so we thought, even though we never had any fish to show for our efforts. Looking back, I am sure our parents were not really that easily taken in, but we liked to think they were. It was after one of these outings that we were both given our first hard lesson about life as it can be, and that particular homecoming was a sad moment indeed.

We were about fourteen years old now and had been, genuinely this time, on a fishing trip which had yielded a good catch of which we were rightly proud. All ready to show off our haul, we had arrived back at Joel's home, where there seemed to be only panic and consternation everywhere, with strangers round the house and Joel's mother in tears. It seemed that shortly after our departure, his father had collapsed complaining of pains in his chest and, before the doctor had arrived to help, he had died in his wife's arms. All was in disarray in Joel's house that evening, and what we had hoped to be a triumphant homecoming had become a tragedy. Joel and his mother were not to be consoled that night, their future, without husband and father, bleak.

My parents and I were much saddened at their loss, for both families were very good friends, and, in the way tragedy sometimes does, the death made the friendship even stronger. Joel now became his mother's strongest support, for even at his tender age he knew, and accepted, where his duty now lay. The years had gone by, and we both grew up, Joel eventually taking over his father's old job as the village cobbler, and I going on to work for a local builder. All the while, our friendship never wavered and my respect for Joel's mother became strong, so bravely had she faced the loss of her husband when her son was young. There were occasions when her advice was sought, given, and much appreciated.

I turned restlessly in my half-sleep, happy at the thought of those days when we were growing up, but then my mind took me back to the events of today, and what had led to them. We were both now twenty-two years old, and at last beginning to make some headway in our working lives. It's strange, isn't it, how fate so often seems to take a hand and upset things just when they are starting to go the way you want. Joel had never been a particularly robust man, healthy enough but not the sort to worry about physique, and now he had developed a strange sort of fever, which no-one could understand. All the efforts of the doctor, with his medicines and potions, were of no avail, and the sickness worsened. Concerned that his work was all that he and his mother had to keep them, Joel struggled to carry on, but soon had to admit defeat, and stopped working in the hope that rest would do the trick. But no, things became steadliy worse, and then one evening as he came in from the workshop, he lay down, slept, and died.

His distraught mother had, with much help, made all the necessary arrangements for his funeral, and for a reception afterwards to which all his family and friends were invited. Half asleep now, I recalled the funeral service and my dread of letting down my old friend as we four pall-bearers prepared to carry him to his last resting place alongside his father. The little procession was well on its sad way, I think. My sleepy mind was clouding my memory. Across the Square we were going, when a small party of men approached us, led by a youngish man whose face was the most striking I had ever seen. He had a look of such nobility of character. He enquired about the procession, and someone explained to him the circumstances, and how the dead man's mother was a widow, now left entirely on her own.

I thought to myself, 'Who is this man who has come into my dream like this? Doesn't he know what we are about?'

At that, the man laid his hand on the bier on which lay Joel's body, stood silent for a moment, and drew back.

At once Joel awoke, and got up, and ran into his mother's arms, smiling all the while.

The man and his friends withdrew, and left this happy moment to the assembled mourners – and at that I awoke, to find my mother standing by me bed, saying, 'Simon, Simon, what is wrong? You are shouting in your sleep. Wake up, son, wake up. Everything's all right now.'

'But I have just had the strangest dream,' I shouted. 'I've just dreamt that Joel is alive and well, and yet we buried him today.'

My mother cried with joy. 'No, Simon. You're not dreaming at all, for yesterday the most wonderful thing occurred here in Nain. Joel really was brought back to life by the touch of the preacher from Nazareth, the man they call Jesus, and even now is waiting downstairs wanting to see you. Get up. Come and see for yourself. You have had no dream, but merely remembered what took place in the Square.'

In a daze, I got up and went downstairs, and there to my joy and amazement was Joel, my friend, my dear old friend. 'But how?' I asked him, bewildered.

'It can only be by the grace of God,' said Joel, 'for yesterday I was dead, but today, after Jesus came, I am alive.'

We hugged one another, joyful and disbelieving, for such an event had no explanation. And yet, as I thought about this momentous happening, there had to be an explanation. I had seen Joel's life, and then his death, and now his life – again.

'How is that possible?' I asked myself. 'Who is this Jesus that he can make my friend live again?' The only conclusion I could think of was too awesome even to consider. 'Has this Jesus shown me the way to a life hereafter?'

BOY – WANTED

'He then took a little child...' Mark, ix, 36

I suppose all of us, from time to time, have one of those days when nothing seems to go right – or at least not as we would like it to go. A day when things go wrong from the very start. When you slip getting out of bed and stub your toe. When all your clothes seem to be outside-in – and you know that you folded them properly the night before. When the water gets spilt over everything but yourself when trying to wash. When the toast is burnt and the milk has gone sour. Oh, a hundred and one things which seem to come together for the sole purpose of upsetting your otherwise tidy arrangements for the day.

That sort of time is bad enough to bear when you are old enough to realise that such days do occur, but, at the same time, know that with some care – and a lot of patience – tomorrow can, and probably will, be better. Now put yourself in the position of a small boy of, say, six, and think how he might feel in the same circumstances. Frustration arising mainly from inexperience would be huge, and then, fed up with everything and everybody round you, you react with tantrums or worse. That of course has the outcome of making all the adults, even your mother, annoyed with you – and their annoyance only makes you feel even more fed up. At six years old it is difficult to recognise the problem.

And that describes exactly how Joseph felt by the middle of that morning. He was thoroughly fed up with everything – and his mother was fed up with him. Not the best recipe for a successful day, not at all. It started when he knocked his bowl of washing water all over the floor. That made him late for breakfast, and in his rush to make up he managed to knock the milk jug off the table. His mother was not pleased, but at least his father had gone to work and missed both catastrophes.

So now he had to do all the clearing up after breakfast, and a broken plate – 'But it just slipped, Mum' – added to his woes. Told to carry the washing basket into the yard, some of the clean washing fell to the earth. Oh dear, more trouble! Now his mother was fed up too, and mostly with Joseph, because she was trying to get off early to the market to buy the week's supply of food and so miss the crowds which always built up by mid-morning, but now, with all these mishaps delaying her, she would probably end up in among the throng at each and every stall she visited. 'Oh,' she muttered in her frustration, 'oh, that boy!'

'That boy,' Joseph, had two elder brothers who were away from home at the moment, and a little sister who was only three. Joseph missed his brothers, thought himself too old for playing with his sister and so was feeling a bit lonely that morning. And to make matters worse, everything seemed to be going wrong. His mother was busy, as all mothers of a young family always are, and this morning she too was having a bad time. Her husband had gone off to work as usual, and the little one had had a disturbed night. She could have done with the help of her two other sons, but they were both away on a trip, so she was left to cope on her own. Her mood was not improved by Joseph spilling water and breaking plates. It was not that she didn't love the little chap, but the events of the morning were getting her down for once, and Joseph just happened to be in the line of fire.

'Right,' she said to Joseph, 'now you can try and do something useful and come with me to the market and help carry my basket.' Those words spelled horror for Joseph, for there was nothing he disliked more than the weekly trip to the market. Shopping for food and other dull household things bored him to tears. He hated it – although, of course, he never refused the food that was provided – and always hoped that somehow he could escape to play with his friends before the summons came. There was no such hope today, though his performance so far today, most of which was totally accidental, had put him right out of favour, and now not only would he be denied his playtime with the other lads, but would have to suffer being dragged round stall after stall while his mother bargained with the merchants. And all his friends would see him, which made things much, much worse. Would nothing go right today? Didn't anybody love him?

Joseph and his mother, with his sister, walked the mile or so into the centre of Capernaum, each carrying a large empty basket, for there was much to be bought. As his mother had feared, the market was packed by the time they reached it, with milling crowds round all the stalls. 'Why,' she said to herself, 'is the biggest crowd always round the stall I need to go to?' If that weren't bad enough, now she had to keep an extra wide eye open for Joseph as they went the rounds, bargaining for the best deal they could get. Their baskets got fuller, and heavier, as the morning proceeded.

With one basket full to the top, they stopped at one corner of the Square for a moment's rest. Joseph sat down on the pavement, weary and thoroughly fed up. His mother took pity on the little fellow and said, 'Look. You stay here with this full basket while I go and finish the shopping with your sister. Now, whatever you do, don't wander away from this spot, and mind the basket. I won't be long.' And with that she was off.

Joseph relaxed and was really quite happy to be left alone for a moment. It was a relief to be by himself, because that way nothing else could go wrong on this horrid day.

He soon grew bored, sitting doing nothing, and looked round for some distraction. Quite nearby, was a group of men who were sitting round and talking – or rather being talked to by one of their number. Joseph dragged the basket closer to the group and stood listening to what was being said. The speaker, a man with a kind face, was going on about how people should behave. Joseph was not really interested in such grown-up talk, but listening helped to pass the time while he waited for his mother. Then he got a surprise, for the man suddenly beckoned to him, with a smile.

Joseph hadn't had a smile all day, and, pulling his basket with him, he went over to the group.

The man smiled again and put his arm round Joseph's shoulder. To the other men he said, 'Anyone who welcomes a little child in my name, welcomes me; and anyone who welcomes me, welcomes not me but the one who sent me.'

The men looked surprised, even puzzled, by these words, but Joseph, who didn't begin to understand what it all meant, was delighted. On this awful day of mishap, here was someone – and a total stranger at that – who actually seemed to want him. And, even more than that, was telling others to do the same. The whole day changed in that moment. No longer was he unwanted. Quite unwittingly, he had found a friend, a man who said welcome and who seemed to mean it.

The kindly man, called 'Master' by his friends, gave Joseph a reassuring hug, and just at that moment Joseph saw his mother coming back across the square.

'I have to go,' he said and ran off, pulling his basket behind him. He beamed at his mother with real pleasure, for his whole day had brightened. He blurted out to her what had just happened, and what the man called 'Master' had said.

His mother laughed as Joseph explained how miserable he had been and said, 'You silly boy. Of course you are wanted and loved by us all. Did it really take a stranger to show you that?' And she gave him a big hug.

As they walked home together, Joseph thought about what that man had said about welcoming little children, and even at his tender age realised that those words had changed his whole day. What a wonderful thing, he thought, that anyone could change your whole day with just a few simple words.

MAN AND A DONKEY

'*... you will find a tethered colt.*' Mark, xi, 2

It was late on Thursday evening and all the talk in the bar of the inn in Bethphage was about the strange events of the week. Ever since the previous Sunday, the whole of Jerusalem had been alive with stories about this man, Jesus, the son of a carpenter some said, who came from Nazareth and had set the town aflame with his preaching of some very novel ideas on God and life and death. There were many who condemned his notions as blasphemous, but he had attracted a small band of loyal followers nonetheless, and opinions were very divided about what he had been saying in such a public way.

The customers in the bar that night all had their own view as the discussions raged for and against, and the landlord was a little concerned lest things should get out of hand. Voices were being raised as opinions hardened, and anyone who had a new thought was either listened to or howled down as he put his view forward. The bar was very noisy, much more than usual, but it was good for business thought the landlord, so he decided to let matters take their course for a little longer. No need, yet, to clear the premises. After all, all this talking made for thirsty throats!

Over in one corner one small group was listening to one of the regulars, a man called Abel, who was telling of his own odd experiences of the past week, experiences which he thought were not unconnected with all the current fuss.

Then suddenly, the door burst open and in came one of the locals who had just got home from the city. 'Quiet!' he yelled, 'And listen! I'll tell you this, they've only arrested him, and taken him off for a hearing. Soldiers and all. Took him in the gardens, they did, and one of his pals gave him away. No one knows what has happened to him since, but I expect we'll all find out tomorrow. I mean, they'll have to do something tomorrow, 'cos the next day's the Sabbath.'

The bar went silent as the company took in this fresh news, but only for a moment. Then the hubbub started again with even greater fervour, and Abel's companions demanded to hear more from him. Abel drew breath and began his story, which had puzzled him all week.

It had all begun last Friday, the day before the Sabbath, when he was getting ready to go home after work. His boss came to him at the gate and said, 'Abel, I have a job for you to do first thing on Sunday morning. Nothing strenuous, but I have agreed to do a favour for some friends. It's about Ferus, the donkey. You know, the unbroken brute who won't let anyone ride him.'

Abel was not impressed, for he and Ferus had had one or two quite violent encounters, and Abel had felt the weight of Ferus's hooves more than once. 'What do you want me to do with him?' asked Abel doubtfully. 'I'm not going to try and break him, not again, 'cos last time he nearly broke me!'

'No, no,' said his boss. 'All you have to do is lead him down to the corner of the lane and tether him to the gate. Then just wait until someone comes to collect him and take him away.'

'But how will I know the right man?' said Abel. 'What's his name?'

'I don't know,' said the boss, 'but he will say he comes from the Master. Don't ask me any more questions because I don't know any more than that, but I've been asked for a favour, so just do it. Right?'

'Anything you say,' said Abel, 'and if I'm seeing the back of Ferus I'm certainly not complaining. Ugly brute he is.'

So, as ordered, early on the Sunday morning Abel went to work and led Ferus off to the end of the lane, but he was puzzled and a bit suspicious of these strange instructions for it was not like his boss to do something for nothing like this. As a safeguard, then, Abel took a workmate with him because he didn't want any trouble afterwards if this odd business went awry somehow. The two of them, with Ferus in tow, went off down the lane, tethered the donkey to a gate and settled down to wait, for Abel had been given no time for the collection.

They had waited perhaps half an hour, when two men appeared, coming from outside the town, and without a word went over to the gate and began to untether Ferus. Abel called out, 'Hey there! Who are you? What are you doing?'

One of the strangers turned and said, 'It's all right, my friend, I come from the Master. Thank you for meeting us.' And with that, the two walked off with Ferus, for once placid, behind.

'Well,' said Abel to his companion 'That's exactly what the boss said would happen, so I suppose it's all right, and you saw what happened.'

And so the pair of them went back up the lane to start their proper day's work. But it was all very odd just the same.

A little later, while they were having their morning

break, they heard a terrific commotion coming from the main road at the end of the lane where they had handed Ferus over. The noise went on, and overcome with curiosity Abel went out to see what was going on. He was staggered at what he saw on the road.

A large crowd, huge almost, was going along the road, all shouting and waving palms and strewing them all over the road. There were shouts of, 'Hosanna, hosanna! Hail to the Master. Hail to Jesus!' There were men, women and quite a number of children all rushing about in a state of high excitement. The noise was tremendous, and people were coming out of their houses, first to see, and then to join in this inexplicable procession.

Abel drew near – and stopped in his tracks, for there, in the middle of all this commotion, was Ferus! But even stranger, Ferus was being ridden. Ferus? Being ridden? 'That is not possible. Ferus is unrideable,' said Abel, aloud, for he was very shaken at the sight, and especially when he looked at the rider.

From his own bitter experience of Ferus, Abel knew that that donkey needed a strong man to control him, someone who knew about breaking and riding, but when he looked at the rider... 'That just cannot be,' he said.

Astride Ferus was the gentlest-looking man, yet with a face of real character, that he had ever seen in his life. He was smiling and waving to the crowd surrounding him, but with no apparent difficulty at controlling a donkey which Abel knew as a brute, who would buck and kick if anyone even looked like trying to ride him.

Abel stood wondering at the sight as the procession went on its way. He just could not understand it, and went back to his work, his thoughts in turmoil. It wasn't until later in the day that he suddenly remembered that the crowd had been calling the rider 'Master'. 'Master,' he said. 'Hey, wait a minute. That's who I was told had

Ferus collected this morning. And that crowd had a name for him, too. Jesus, they called him. Yes, that's right, Jesus.'

One of Abel's listeners broke in on his story, saying, 'But that's the name of this preacher from Nazareth who's been arrested this evening. He's the one who has been causing all the uproar in the city all week, with his talk of love and peace and being kind to your neighbour.'

Abel was trying to collect his thoughts to make some sense of what he had seen last Sunday and of what was happening in the city now. He was very confused, very confused indeed. Abel knew about animals, more perhaps than he knew about people, and he was sure that this man, Jesus, had some special gift if he could subdue a brute like Ferus – and in so short a time. How then, could a man with such soothing powers possibly be a rabble-rouser, as some were describing him? The two things just didn't add up – or did they?

'When you think about it,' said Abel to his audience, 'the way he was able to make that donkey so amenable does square with all his talk of peace and love, doesn't it? But what he has been saying upsets the powers-that-be because it goes against all they hold to be right, so of course they're upset. Think about it. I mean, any man that can pacify old Ferus must be a bit special, so why shouldn't he do the same for all of us? There may be something in what he says, after all. Funny isn't it? I never had any time for that Ferus but, wow, has he made me think.'

THE WATER CARRIER

'... a man carrying a pitcher of water.'
Luke, xxii, 10

Adam was a quiet, unassuming man in his early fifties, who lived with his wife and family in a small house towards the outskirts of the Jerusalem. He had worked all his life for the same employer who ran a provisions business in the centre of the city, and whose customers were many and varied. Adam was responsible for ensuring that orders got to the right address in good condition and over the years had proved his worth, as shown by the number of satisfied clients on the books. When not in the store putting orders together, much of his day was spent out delivering orders, sometimes on the donkey-cart but quite often on foot, when things were particularly busy. Reflective by nature, this time on the road gave him plenty of opportunity to think and so he had an opinion on most of the problems of the times. He was, indeed, something of a philosopher in his own quiet way.

These past few days had been anything but quiet, however, as the whole city prepared for the Day of Passover. The demands on Adam were many and seemingly endless as he toiled in his dedicated way to satisfy all his customers. The whole city throbbed with activity as preparations went ahead, as, in addition to the local inhabitants, many visitors had been thronging into the city well in advance of the day itself. Most of these incomers were, of course, perfectly bona fide visitors who had come for the legitimate purpose of celebration of the feast, but inevitably there were some among their number whose intent was not so good. These latter were nothing but trouble as they went about looking for illicit gain, and with no hesitation of resorting to robbery and thuggery if, in their nasty minds, such activity was the only way to make their ill-gotten profit. As the week proceeded things got worse and there had been reports of marauding gangs in certain parts of the city. Such men of bad intent always seem to be present when and wherever large assemblies come together for good purpose, and this week had been no exception. As a result, there was a distinct atmosphere of tension in the city.

This week, too, there was an added ingredient in the situation. There were stories going the rounds of a travelling preacher from Nazareth who had been stirring matters up with his strange utterings. His teachings had upset the authorities to a great degree on more than one occasion, running counter – or so it seemed – to the more orthodox views set out in the Law. Added to the already hectic situation, the arrival of this man, Jesus, was yet another facet of the life of the city. None of it made Adam's task any easier, although on his travels round the town he had come across this preacher on two occasions and had heard something of what the man was saying. In his own quiet way, Adam was quite impressed by what he heard, and had been turning these new ideas over in his mind. Privately, he thought there could not really be much argument against notions of living your life in peace and caring for your fellow man, but he had to admit to some misgivings about the man's claim to be the son of God. That was something to make a man think – and seriously.

As Adam had been going about his business day by day he had given much thought to Jesus and his preaching. He realised fairly quickly, of course, that such a man and his odd ideas presented a threat to the status quo and, so, to the Jewish authorities. He had no trouble whatsoever in accepting the basis provided by the Commandments given to Moses on the mountain. Oh, no. He was after all a God-fearing man, but thoughts are funny things and now he was starting to think that perhaps those Commandments were just a basis, a starting point, and not the be-all-and-end-all as contemporary thinking dictated. Perhaps there was more to it than merely sticking to the letter of the Law.

Adam had always had to struggle for what he had, not that he was complaining, for he had a good wife, a loving family and a secure job. Nevertheless, he had a lot of sympathy for these notions of God as a loving God, who cared about people and wanted, expected, people to care about both God and their fellows. He knew that not everybody shared these thoughts of his and, realising that there were some who could make trouble for him, he very wisely kept his thoughts to himself – even from his wife and family.

He was dragged out of his thoughts by the voice of his employer. 'Adam,' he was saying, 'there's one last important order which must go out today. It's a last minute request from my old friend, Raphael, for a large pitcher of water, to be delivered to his upper room for a party of thirteen. Will you make sure that's done without fail and in good time?'

'Of course I will,' said Adam, 'but I'll have to take it myself as the boy is out nearly all day with the cart. I mean, I'll have to carry it there, but it'll get there, don't worry.'

It was not the best news Adam had had that busy day,

and the prospect of carrying a large pitcher of water for some twenty minutes or so, and at his age, was not really attractive. However, work was work, and he went about his preparations.

Aware of the tension in the streets and mindful of his own safety as well as his employer's orders, he worked out his route with some care. He planned to avoid the main streets, and therefore the crowds, as far as possible because, apart from having easier access, he would also run less risk of coming across any of the nastier elements in the crowds. His planned route would be via a number of smaller roads, alleys almost, which were both short and safer. He had a special shoulder pad which he used for such jobs and he now strapped this on, and having filled the large pitcher, hoisted it up, steadied himself, and set off for the house of Raphael.

To reach the first of his short cuts he had first to go along one of the roads coming into the city from outside for about thirty or forty yards, and this he did with no difficulty. As he crossed the road to the first alley, he noticed two men heading for the centre of the city who were quite clearly visitors. They had that look of men from the country in the way they walked and in their dress, and Adam gave them no more than a passing look. Along his short cut he went and soon came to a junction where he had to turn and, for a short distance, almost go back on himself. As he did so, he noticed again the two strangers, now also coming along the first alley.

'I expect they have friends in the city,' Adam thought to himself, 'and if they don't they'll soon get lost in this maze.' He went on, and after a few hundred yards paused to adjust the pitcher on his shoulder, for it was of no mean weight. As he did so, again, there were the two men, now into the second alley behind him. As he stopped, so did they. It was almost as if they were keeping watch on him, which puzzled Adam. Perhaps they were just looking for an address, and were a bit lost.

His load adjusted, Adam walked on. He was now getting quite close to his destination, and a sound behind him made him look round. There were the two men, a little closer now. When Adam stopped, they stopped. Little warning bells were ringing in Adam's mind now, conscious as he was of all the prevalent stories of robbery in the streets this week. Who were these two who quite definitely seemed to be following him? And why? He had no money or valuables with him, only a pitcher of water, and surely that wasn't worth stealing? He quickened his pace as much as he could for the sooner he made his delivery, he felt, the better. He felt decidedly unsafe with these two characters behind him. He took another quick look behind him and to his dismay saw that his unwanted companions were moving faster to keep up with him.

Now thoroughly alarmed and certain that he was about to be the victim of an attack, Adam hurried on, ignoring the weight on his shoulder, anxious only to reach the house of Raphael which was in sight at the next corner. Through the gate and across the courtyard he rushed, almost in panic as the pair followed him right up to the door. Trembling with fright, he fell through the doorway into the house to be greeted by Raphael himself.

'Ah, Adam, how good of you to come so soon.'

Adam, breathless from fright and his exertions, lowered his burden to the floor and gasped out his fears about the two men who had followed him so long. Footsteps caused him to turn round, to find that his pursuers had come in behind him. Adam tensed himself, fearing the worst. Surely they would not attack him now, here in the house?

Now Adam received a great shock, for having greeted him, Raphael went forward and met the two with a smile.

‘Welcome’ he said. ‘I have waited in so that I might show you the upper room, which I have set aside for the Master’s Passover Feast. Come along with me and I will take you to it.’

One of the two spoke to Raphael. ‘Our Master, Jesus, is very grateful for your kindness and asks us to thank you.’ And then he spoke to Adam. ‘The Master said we would find you, and that you would lead us to this house. It has happened exactly as he said it would. You have been an excellent guide to two strangers in your city. Thank you for your help.’

Adam was speechless and stood to one side as the three went up to see the room set aside for the gathering. His thoughts were in turmoil. He was trembling, partly from relief that his fears of the last half hour were ill-founded, partly from sheer amazement at what he had just been told. He could barely credit that his pursuit had been intended. Indeed it had been foreseen and arranged, according to the men, by this Jesus, who had been causing such a stir by his preaching – preaching with which Adam had found so much sympathy.

Adam went home with much to think about, and it was later in the evening, as he sat contemplating all that had happened to him that day, that he began to make some sense of the whole affair. Adam, for all his lowly status, increasingly could see nothing but good in what this Jesus was preaching, whereas the Jewish authorities were suspicious, indeed afraid, of him because his message seemed to go beyond the Law. And in the same way, Adam had been terrified of these two men who had followed him that day, only to discover that they were friends and messengers of the very man whose teachings Adam was beginning to think were so right.

Adam was at peace in his mind as he recognised the whole irony of the day’s events. Just as the authorities had misjudged Jesus, he, Adam, had misjudged his messengers. It all went to show how wildly misleading appearances can be.

RUN FOR COVER

'. . . and he ran away naked.' Mark, xiv, 52

One of the aims of any father must surely be to ensure, as far as he is able, that his son is given the best possible basis for a secure, and hopefully prosperous, future. To that end, then, he will strive to educate, to set a good example and to provide the opportunity for gaining experience which will prepare his son for life beyond the parental home. Dermid's father was no exception to such a course and had done all that he could to provide good tutors for his son against the background of a settled home life. At his father's wish, Dermid was about to move on and embark on the next stage of the programme which his father had so carefully arranged for him.

Dermid was just eighteen years old, a well-mannered and well-read young man, who was destined, so his father hoped, to succeed to the running of the family business which had been built up over years of hard work. His future was assured and his father was quietly pleased with this young man who showed every sign of having inherited the acumen necessary for a successful career. His father was a wealthy merchant, well-respected in and beyond Capernaum, who had a reputation for fair dealing and probity, and he had arranged for Dermid to go to the city and spend a year or so gaining experience in the world. On his return, the intention was that Dermid would take over the day-to-day running of the business, so allowing his father to enjoy well-earned retirement.

All arangements in place, Dermid was enjoying a few days' holiday at home, spending his time saying farewell to friends, and this involved an amount of travelling in the countryside surrounding Capernaum. It was, understandably, a time of mixed emotions for all, particularly so for Dermid since he was the one who was going off, as far as he was concerned, into a world unknown. He was excited at the prospect, and looked forward to meeting new people, hearing new things and seeing new sights. He had, at the same time, some apprehension about the venture, but he was a dutiful son who realised and appreciated all that his father was doing for him.

And so it happened, one morning, whilst returning from the home of a family with whom he had spent the previous night, that, some miles west of Capernaum, Dermid fell in with a large crowd assembled round the base of a hill and being addressed by a man of about thirty, who from his speech was a fellow-Galilean. He was speaking in a firm way, not in a bullying way but certainly in a tone of some authority. Intrigued at finding such a gathering out here in the country, Dermid stopped to listen, both from sheer curiosity and as a way of giving his pony a rest. Some in the crowd were showing dissent at what the speaker was saying, but he was answering their queries in a firm, yet gentle, way.

'Who is this man?' asked Dermid of his immediate neighbour.

'His name is Jesus and he comes from Nazareth. You must have heard of him, surely, for he has been around for a year now, preaching his message of love of God and man.'

On reflection Dermid did recall something about this man with strange ideas who was regarded in some circles as a nuisance – and in others as a danger. Dermid thought that he should take advantage of his chance meeting and see what this fellow had to say. He sat down with the others to listen and was truly amazed at what he heard. So interested did he become that he lost all track of time, until he realised from the position of the sun in the sky how late it had become.

The crowd was starting to disperse now, and Dermid, knowing that his parents would be worried if he didn't return when expected, began his journey home. It was almost dark when he came to his house to find his mother anxious for his safety. His father, too, was concerned and wanted to know where he had been all this time, especially when Dermid said that he was tired and hungry as he had left his friend's home that morning.

'But what on earth have you been doing? Where have you been that has made you so late? We've both been worried sick,' said his father, while his mother was telling the servants to bring food and drink for the weary traveller.

'Father,' said Dermid, when he managed to get a word in, 'I have been hearing the most incredible and wonderful things from that travelling preacher they call Jesus.'

'What things?' said his father, a tone of distrust in his voice, for he had heard something of this man in the course of his business dealings.

'I can't remember all he said, but these were the important points. He said "Blessed are the poor in spirit; theirs is the Kingdom of Heaven. Blessed are the meek; they shall possess the land. Blessed are they that mourn; they shall be comforted. Blessed are they that hunger and thirst after justice; they shall have their fill. Blessed are the merciful; they shall obtain mercy. Blessed are the clean of heart; they shall see God. Blessed are the peacemakers; they shall be called the children of God. Blessed are they that suffer persecution for justice sake; theirs is the Kingdom of Heaven." I've never heard anything so marvellous in all my life. Don't you think so, Father?'

Dermid was not pleased at his father's reply.

'Dermid,' he said, 'I've never heard such rubbish. These things are no basis for a businessman. You won't last five minutes with ideas like that, I can tell you. Oh, no, my boy. The Law of Moses is good enough for me, and my father before me, so just forget this crazy talk. There's nothing in it. Nothing at all.'

There was a strained silence for a moment, and then the arguments began. They raged on for hours, but Dermid's father was adamant. Dermid must do what had been arranged, go to Jerusalem, and forget all about 'blessed this and blessed that'. Or else! Much subdued, Dermid spent a most unhappy night, but by morning he had become the dutiful, but now somewhat disillusioned, son once more. Two days later he left his father's house and went off to meet the world.

The next year passed swiftly for Dermid, for there was much to do and learn as he struggled to live up to his father's expectations and acquire the skills he needed. He was doing very well, too, and his mentor thought he showed great promise, so much so that he had despatched him about some business away from the city. It was on this journey that Dermid again met – as Dermid knew him – the 'Blessed man' – preaching as ever to a crowd. Today, though, he message was more difficult to understand and accept, for it was to do with family relationships.

Jesus was saying, 'Do you think I came to give peace upon the earth? No! I tell you, but division. For henceforth in one house five will be divided ... father against son and son against his father.'

As he heard these words, Dermid's mind went back to that noisy argument they had had. Was this really what was happening to him, he wondered. He still recalled so clearly the words this man had used that day on the hill – and still had them in his heart.

Dermid went back to the city that night, confused at the mixture of thought and emotion he was experiencing. This was not the experience his father had intended for him in the city, but deep down he knew that he must, with great reluctance, even pain, go against his father's views. Several times over the ensuing weeks Dermid contrived to hear more from this wonderful speaker, and was the more convinced by what he said even when he demanded that his followers should go 'without purse or haversack and with no spare tunic'.

And then came that day, the Sunday before Passover, when the Master, as Dermid had come to know him, entered Jerusalem amidst untold celebration and welcome from the people. All that week, Dermid was always there, on the fringe of the crowd, watching and listening to the Master's words. Excitement grew with every day, and excitement became tension, until inevitably the authorities stepped in. There was talk of uprising and division, and then, on the evening of Passover Day, the Master was confronted by soldiers and guards in the gardens. Suddenly, Judas, whom Dermid had actually met, stepped forward and kissed the Master. Soldiers now grasped him – and all was tumult!

It was time to get out of here, thought Dermid, and with all the others rushed for the gates, harried by the soldiers. In the heat of the evening, Dermid was wearing only a light linen garment, and as he struggled to get through the press, he was grabbed roughly by a soldier, who wrestled to hold him. To his horror, in the violent struggle, the linen garment was ripped from his body with great force, leaving Dermid absolutely naked. In total embarassment and fear, Dermid fled into the comparative freedom of the streets with only one aim in mind – to get away from this awful place and hide himself in the safety of his lodgings. In the peace of his own room, he thought with shame of what he had done. He had deserted the Master at the time of decision, and over the next few days his remorse grew and grew as the events of the week unfolded. The climax of that week was too terrible to contemplate as Dermid fought to find solace.

His distraught mind kept taking him back to that afternoon on the hill a year ago, when he had first heard words he now treasured. He thought often of the warning about the family divided among itself. And he recalled the strictures about having 'no purse, no haversack, and NO SPARE TUNIC'.

All these things seemed to apply directly to him, especially the bit about having no spare tunic. But, surely, he thought, it went much further than having no tunic. Surely, the real point was that in his hour of panic he, Dermid, had lost not only his clothes, but had deprived himself of the protection of the Master as he had, in terror, run for cover!

MY COUSIN, MALCHUS

'*. . . a relation of the man.*' John, xviii, 26

Tobias came home that Friday evening exhausted, mentally and physically. What a day it had been! In fact, come to that, the whole week had been pretty lively. Ever since last Sunday when that fellow, Jesus, – Master, his followers called him – had arrived in Jerusalem hardly a day had passed without some crisis or other. Tobias and all his colleagues in the service of the high priest, Caiaphas, were in the same state of weariness, having spent the last five days rushing here, there and everywhere as they tried to keep pace with the demands which had been put upon them all. Today, though, had been by far the worst, for most of the staff of the house had been up half the night following the man's arrest in the gardens last evening. Tobias was having great trouble trying to get all that had happened straight in his mind. What with Jesus' arrest, his appearance first in front of the Sanhedrin, then before the Roman governor, Pilate, and then, finally, his last journey to Golgotha for his crucifixion, it had all been too much. At least, Tobias thought, now that the man was dead the affair was over once and for all. Things could only improve from now on.

As he sat and revelled in the luxury of just being able to sit down for a moment in the peace and quiet of his own quarters within the high priest's house, his thoughts turned to two very odd incidents which had occurred during the last twenty-four hours. The first of these had involved his cousin, Malchus, more than a little, and painfully at that. He must go over and see Malchus to make sure that he was all right after his ordeal during the arrest. Now that he thought about it, that incident when Malchus had been injured was strange in the extreme, frightening almost, and with no simple explanation. Had what he had seen last evening really happened? He cast his mind back to the scene.

Tobias and Malchus were cousins, and both in the service of the high priest, whom they had served loyally for some time, Tobias as valet, and Malchus as bodyguard. That was why they had both been so involved this last week, and had been present last night when that fellow, Judas, had given his friend in to the hands of the authorities. It had not been a pleasant sight to see a man betrayed by a friend, even when the betrayed had been causing so much upset in the city and beyond. The arrest had been quite carefully planned, and had been carried out last night by soldiers and servants of the high priest. Tobias had been present, on the fringe of the crowd, more as an observer than an active participant and had seen what happened very clearly.

Jesus and his followers had been in the garden when the soldiers arrived, and, as arranged, Judas had come forward and greeted his master very ostentatiously with a kiss, saying, 'Hail, Rabbi.'

That had been the signal for the arrest to be made, and as the soldiers moved in and took hold of their man, one of his friends, known as Peter, had drawn his sword and with a swift blow had severed poor Malchus' ear. It fell to the ground, blood pouring everywhere, and it was then that the most weird thing had happened.

Jesus, in custody, had rebuked Peter strongly, which

might have been expected from one who preached peace, but also in one quick movement had touched Malchus on his wounded head – and there, for all to see, his ear was restored, apparently unharmed.

Peter had by now put his sword back into its scabbard, and with all the activity going on, the soldiers shouting, and the crowd, now alarmed, trying to make a swift departure, this unbelievable incident had been lost in the chaos of the moment. Maybe because it all happened so quickly, many of the crowd did not even see what occurred, but Tobias saw, and Malchus most certainly did. It was as if that ear had been restored by magic, by some strange power!

The rest of the night was a flurry of endless activity, as the centre of the action shifted first to the house of Annas, and then on to that of Caiaphas, where the preliminary investigation had been carried out. It was during this examination that the second strange incident of the night took place, and, as with the first, that man, Peter, had been involved, but this one had also concerned Tobias himself. It had occurred towards the end of a very long night, almost morning in fact, when Tobias had gone out from the house into the courtyard to refresh himself in the cold air of the dawn. There was a fire there and round it a small crowd of people waiting around to hear the latest news at the end of a turbulent night. Some of the other servants and maids from the household were there too, and Tobias went over to join them. As he neared the group, he saw to his surprise that that fellow, Peter, who had struck Malchus so violently last evening, was standing in the group, warming himself at the fire.

'What a cheek he has,' said Tobias to himself, 'standing there like that.' He noticed one or two of the others speak to Peter, who was seen to shake his head vigorously as if in denial of something. In some irritation at the man's presence there, Tobias went over and said to him, 'Weren't you with him last night in the garden? I'm sure I saw you there with your sword, didn't I?'

To his surprise his accusation was met with a vehement denial. 'No, I was not!' said Peter, and turned away. Just then, with dawn breaking, a cock crowed in the distance, the call coming over clearly in the thin morning air. The effect on Peter was dramatic. It was as if he had been struck forcibly, so sudden was his reaction – and, to Tobias, what a very strange reaction. Tobias had never seen such an instant and dramatic change in a man. But why? So a cock crowed! What was there about that to make a man collapse?

Peter reeled away, his face contorted in anguish, tears pouring down his face, and muttering audibly, 'He said I would deny him. And I have!'

Tobias pondered on this now. 'What could Peter have meant?' Tobias said to himself. 'Surely he didn't mean that Peter had been forewarned that he would react like that to the cock-crow, did he? No, of course he didn't. And yet...' It was time, thought Tobias, to cease this line of thinking or he might start to believe it, and that was dangerous thinking. He decided to go over and see Malchus, for although his wound appeared to have been cured last night – there's that dangerous thinking again – he must have suffered some trauma from such an odd, inexplicable event, and anyway it would do them both good to talk about it all. It would get all this nonsense out of their systems, he hoped. So off he went and found Malchus resting in his quarters, very tired but none the worse for his experience. Physically, at least. Sure enough, the ear showed no sign of any damage whatsoever, but both of them had seen it on the ground one minute and back, unharmed, the next. No matter how they looked at the affair, there was no earthly explanation. What were they saying, they asked each other, what? Dangerous thinking?

To change the subject, Tobias now related the strange story of what had taken place in the courtyard when the cock crowed, and what he had heard Peter mutter to himself. That started them both thinking all over again.

'You know,' said Malchus, 'that Peter is an odd character, isn't he? I mean, one minute he's hitting me with his sword and taking my ear off. No, don't start all that again! But then, you say, he's in tears and totally overwrought at the crow of a cock, muttering that it was all foretold by this Jesus. It gets weirder and weirder, the more you think of it. First he's violent and his master subdues him with a word, and then he's in tears. I tell you, Tobias, it's all beyond me, and that's the truth!'

They both sat quiet for a while, these events and thoughts whirling round in their heads. Then Malchus broke the silence. 'Anyway, it's all over now. It was all finished this afternoon when they nailed him to that cross. There's no Peter and no cock-crow can change that. It's over.'

Tobias, deep in thought, looked up, with concern on his face. 'I'm sure you're right, Malchus,' he said, 'but there's one thing that still bothers me, knowing what we've seen. We've both heard of his miracles and prophecies – and we both now know from last night that they happen. What worries me is that this Jesus also said he would rise from the dead after three days. Today's Friday, three days takes us to Sunday, and, well, I just can't help wondering . . . ?'

A FACE IN THE CROWD

'. . . *and of women too.*' Luke, xxiii, 28

When Anna woke up in the morning, her first thoughts were of the happy family gathering the previous evening, when in accordance with the Law and custom she and her whole family had celebrated the beginning of the Feast of Unleavened Bread in the traditional way, and she was pleased that everything had gone so well. With her husband, son and two daughters she had shared the meal, and had enjoyed being able to relax for once without the usual mundane, annoying distractions which were wont to disturb other family meals during the year. It was good to sit and talk, about family matters, about the careers of the children – no longer children indeed, but young adults now – in fact, about anything and everything under the sun. Lovely just to sit and enjoy one another's company. How fortunate we are, she thought. It had been a splendid evening and she was pleased.

Mind you, there had been moments when there was anything but full agreement round the table, especially when money or politics came up, but any disagreement had been, on the whole, good-hearted and without rancour of any kind. Only one subject had brought forth some varied and strongly-held views, and that was when her husband had mentioned the arrival of this man, Jesus, in the city on the previous Sunday. He had made his entrance on a donkey, and had been welcomed by many of his cheering supporters as if he were royalty. Since then the stories about him had spread like wildfire, and there was much gossip about his activities. There were reports of him performing miracles, some even saying that he had raised people from the dead, but the real talking-point was about his two extraordinary claims. Rumour had it that he had claimed to be the Son of God, and if that were not enough, that he would rise to life again three days after his death.

Opinions round Anna's table were varied. Her two daughters both thought the man must be crazy to make such claims, while her husband seemed to regard him as nothing more than a nuisance and a rabble-rouser. All three thought it best to ignore him and his odd ideas. Her son, on the other hand, was ready to give him a hearing, with his talk of 'love your neighbour', and said he should at least be allowed to say his piece, even if some did think he was a crank. 'Go on! Live and let live,' said her son.

Anna kept her own counsel, happy just that her family were round her and in such lively mood. The exchange of such varied and strongly-held opinions, expressed so freely round her table had, at the same time, given Anna to reflect on the irony that talking about religion, no matter how loosely, should produce such animated differences. After all, she felt, should not religion be a means of bringing together? If pressed, she would probably have agreed with her son's feelings about this preacher.

Her son was now thirty-two years old, still unmarried, and made pottery which he managed to sell with some success. Meeting all sorts in his working life, he had a sensible head on his shoulders, and usually showed a willingness to listen to others first rather than making hasty decisions. His mother thought the world of him, not that she favoured him unduly, for she loved her daughters dearly, but her son had shown great courage in making his own way in business and she was proud of his success. With some satisfaction, then, Anna began the new day and had much to do, for tomorrow was the Sabbath and there were some outstanding preparations to be completed.

As her family got ready for the day, there was some talk of the noisy disturbance in the streets the previous night as they had been retiring to bed, and they all wondered what could have been the cause on such a special day in the calendar. With family departed, Anna set out for the market to get what she needed, and soon began to hear of the trouble in the Garden when this man, Jesus, had been arrested. It seemed that the opinion of the authorities had been much stronger than any expressed at table on the previous evening, and the man was now being investigated by the high priest and the Roman governor. The gossip in the market was that the majority of the people were against him, and his future did not look at all good. As Anna went about the market, there was certainly an unfamiliar, almost unhealthy, buzz about the whole city, and an atmosphere of brooding anticipation as the decision on his future was awaited from the Sanhedrin.

About mid-morning, with most of her purchases made, Anna was making her way back towards home in the very busy streets. The crowds were quite normal for the city was host to many visitors at this paschal time. She was attracted by the clamour of many voices coming from a main street in the city, the street which she knew led from the Governor's Court to the hill, Golgotha, where criminals were executed, and, mindful of the disturbances on the evening before, mingled with the crowd to find out the cause of all the excitement.

The crowd was dense, and, at the spot where she joined it, seemed to be composed largely of women. As Anna brought herself nearer the front, she first saw, showing above the heads of the crowd, what seemed to be a large piece of wood, but as she drew closer she saw that the wood was part of a huge cross. And now she saw the most horrific sight, the worst that she had ever seen in her life. So great was the shock, she halted, stock still, as she tried to take in the scene before her. As though paralysed she stood, rooted to the spot, her mind denying what her eyes were telling her. 'This cannot be,' she told herself, 'it just cannot be!' But her eyes did not deceive her!

Bowed down under the weight of that cross, she saw a man, totally exhausted by his effort to carry such a burden. But what a man! Exhausted, yes, but a figure of such pain and misery as she could never have imagined. His back bleeding from the welts of a whip, his head encased in what appeared to be a crown made of plaited thorn twigs, he struggled to walk, no, to stagger towards that awful place, Golgotha. In spite of the terrible agony he must have been suffering, there was yet a look of nobility about his pain-worn face, and, even as she watched, Anna saw him pause and speak to the women in the crowd. One of them wiped the blood-covered face and his gratitude showed through, despite his pain. And now he even managed to speak! Anna was close enough to hear some of his words, in spite of the constant noise of the crowd.

'Daughters of Jerusalem,' he said, 'weep not for me but for yourselves and for your children. For behold, days are coming in which men will say "Blessed are the barren, and the wombs that never bore, and breasts that . . ." ' His words were lost in the hubbub, but Anna was deeply affected by those she had managed to hear. It was only now that she heard the name, Jesus, mentioned in the blur of noise, and realised in amazement that this poor creature before her must be the preacher about whom so much had been said at her table only last night. She recalled her son's remarks about 'letting him say his piece' and 'live and let live'. But this! And on his way to savage death!

Her eyes went back to the tragic, noble figure under that cross, sick at what she saw. Did anyone deserve such treatment when his only crime, as far as she could see, had been to say what he felt to be right? Were his ideas of how to live and die and worship God really deserving of such inhumanity? Powerless to help and helpless in her pity for him, she could watch this spectacle no longer, so awful was it to her senses. In tears now, she let the macabre procession pass her by, as, with one last despairing glance, she saw again this vision of a man in total agony, and as she looked an awesome thought came to her. The man before her was no older than her son, her own beloved son, and this man too must have a mother. What of her? Was she a witness to this pitiable sight?

That was the moment Anna came to know the meaning of compassion, for now she thought how she would feel if her dear son were made to suffer such humiliating agony – and all because he preached a message of love. It was surely more than any mother could bear, but somewhere that poor man's mother must know what motherhood meant in all its depth. The pangs of childbirth would be as nothing against such pain-filled loss, and deep-down Anna grieved for Jesus' mother in her heart.

ONE GOOD TURN

'...putting a sponge on a hyssop stick.'
John, xix, 29

Our human race is nothing if not diverse, a baffling mixture of good and bad, of love and hate, of generosity and selfishness, and the wide range of character and personality is almost without limit. There are those who are serious and those who are not so serious. Some, without doubt, are of good intent and others, just as certainly, are not. For some, duty and respect stand large in their approach to life, and such men will have a healthy regard for authority, be that in the form of law or the wishes of their parents. They are happy to conform with the accepted and conventional way of life, training, qualifying, and pursuing a career which makes good use of their own particular talents, and at the same time contributing something to the general good.

The converse, of course, is equally true, and there are those who do not, who will not, conform, and who, having ignored all attempts by others to help, will then go through life bemoaning their lack of success, complaining at their lot and making little or no contribution to society. There are some, too, who quite deliberately turn their talents to wrong-doing, without any thought for others and with a blatant disregard for the rule of law, their avowed intention being to pursue nothing but their own selfish ends, no matter that others may suffer.

Somewhere in between there are yet others who are not dedicated in any particular way, but who at the same time do not have any real evil in them. They always look on the bright side, are quite sure that something will come along to better their lot, and adopt an amazingly casual attitude to everything. They will do just enough to get by and will always be on the look-out for an opening, a chance to make some profit from any situation in which they may find themselves. They will even do a good turn for others, especially if there is some advantage for themselves, but would never knowingly do something out of malice, nor would they ever use violence. They are not, however, totally averse to bending the rules – or the law – if they think they can get away with it.

They are smart and live on their wits, always on the alert and ready to make the quick decision. They have a knack of being in the right place at the right time, and their philosophy is one of 'some you win, some you lose'. They are popular with their immediate acquaintances, but not altogether trusted by them. They are what might be termed 'loveable rogues'.

Amos, or Mozzie to his friends, was such a fellow. Now in his mid-twenties, he had long ago left his father's house and come to Jerusalem, where he was well-known round the city as one who would turn his hand to anything for payment, no questions asked, for he always had an eye to the main chance. He could well have remained at home in Bethany as a young man, where he would have inherited the family shoemaking business, but that was too tame for his wandering spirit, and he had left for the city as soon as he could. Wherever there were people or, better still, a large crowd, there Mozzie was to be found, always on the fringe and with his hand-cart, talking, dealing, offering his services to any one who seemed to need his wide-ranging talents. He was a jack-of-all-trades who was prepared to undertake almost anything and do it well – and if not, always able to talk his way out of trouble. He expected no thanks from anyone – only their cash.

This Passover week was an opportunity without compare, for the crowds in the city were large and demanding. There was always something to carry, to mend, to arrange, to sell or to obtain for somebody, and Mozzie was in his element. He had had a fairly profitable week, too, so much so that he was seriously thinking of spending a weekend of idleness and going home to see his mother. But then, on Passover Day, all sorts of things had started to happen. He had seen the arrest of this man, Jesus, in the Garden that evening, and had followed the crowd for most of the night in the hope of finding something to earn himself a little bonus.

He had gone back to his room for some rest very early in the morning, but not for long. He was not about to miss such a promising situation just because he was tired. Oh, no! And so, there he was, back outside the Governor's Palace just as the cock crew, his little cart piled high today with fruit and some flagons of common wine, known by the better-off as 'people's wine' because of its very sour taste. It was, in fact, over-fermented cider and was little better than vinegar, but on a hot day thirsty men would drink anything. It had cost Mozzie very little and, his profit assured, he was looking forward to today with great hope.

The crowd was already gathering when Mozzie arrived, for news had already spread that things were beginning to move, and it was not long before the Governor appeared, the prisoner at his side, to offer the mob the choice of freeing either him or a notorious thug called Barabbas. There was much shouting and yelling – good for a thirst, thought Mozzie – with everyone now screaming for the preacher to be crucified. The atmosphere was one of mob hysteria, and Mozzie was surprised to say the least when Barabbas was freed to the wild acclaim of the crowds. Mozzie had no thoughts, one way or the other, about this man, Jesus and his preachings, but secretly he had to admit to some doubts about the thug being preferred for release. After all, Barabbas was a known villain, while this other fellow had only been spreading some odd ideas of his own. Still, it was not his problem, and meanwhile there was business to be done.

Some time went by, and then Jesus came out again, but this time burdened by a huge wooden cross, and clearly he had been flogged, for there was blood on his face and back. And on his head there was a sort of crown made from twisted, plaited thorn sticks. He was indeed a sorry sight, and his appearance had the mob baying again as he staggered under that awesome load. Surrounded by his guards, he moved off slowly in the direction of Golgotha, the place of execution, with the crowd following behind as if in some macabre procession. Several times along the way, the condemned man paused, on occasion falling to the ground, his agony plain to see, and all the while the jeers of the crowd went on.

Knowing the destination of the procession, Mozzie went by back ways and short cuts to be there first and gain a good pitch to sell his wares. Once on the hill, his thoughts were turning more and more to this poor tortured man, who suffered with never a word of criticism or condemnation for his tormenters. Mozzie watched in growing horror from close by as the nails were driven through his feet and hands, and the cross was hoisted upright. In the crowd now there was silence, apart from one or two unseemly shouts which served only to draw attention to the strange dignity and nobility of that savage spectacle.

And all at once, there came a voice, a weak and croaking noise. Just two hoarse words were heard. 'I thirst,' said the figure on the cross.

As if stung, Mozzie, the trader, reacted with his usual alacrity, not realising the irony of his position, for had he not come out today to provide wine for the thirsty? He jumped forward, and taking a sponge from the cart, dipped it into one of the flagons of wine and offered it on a stick to the face above him. That pain-ridden face grimaced at him as wine met lips, turned away for a moment, but only a moment, and then looked down. Mozzie had never seen such a face, twisted in its agony, but as he looked he saw such an unforgettable expression in those eyes. There were no words, but those eyes seemed to give out a beam of love in their gratitude. If a look ever said 'Thank you' those eyes did, and eloquently in their silence. The sad head sagged, and a moment Mozzie would never forget was gone.

Mozzie backed away. In all his life, he had never known such a moment. He had never, ever, expected anyone to thank him for his help, only to pay, but this man had expressed such gratitude with just a look. In spite of what he must have been suffering, he had yet found strength and time and love to say 'Thank you' – and for a taste of the most unpalatable wine. Mozzie wandered off the hill, his cart and fruit and wine forgotten. He halted as the sky grew black and thunder rent the air, and, turning to the cross again, wondered in his heart, 'What kind of man was this?'

ONE EVENING, LONG AGO

'. . . and in the Garden, a new tomb.'
John, xix, 41

The life of an innkeeper is always busy. Every day is an endless round of noise and bustle, for there is always the demanding customer to be satisfied, the empty shelf to be refilled, and, importantly, the cellar to be replenished. It is every bit as bad for the landlord's wife who, in addition to her 'front-of-house' involvement in support of her husband, is so often the mother of a family who quite rightly expect her full and undivided attention. Yes, the life of such a couple is, to say the least, very active and therefore very tiring too. But what, then, of their children? It is a very special couple who manage to combine all these activies to achieve both a successful business and a loving home.

Samuel came from just such a home. His memories of home were of parents who provided all that any growing boy could wish for, a place where there was guidance, help, and, most important of all, love in abundance. Samuel had great affection still for that little inn in Bethlehem, where he had been born and had grown up, and often visited to see his parents who still laboured as they always had. They were now of an age when retirement beckoned – Samuel himself was now forty years old – and if they had one regret it must be that their only son had no interest at all in taking over their inn, none whatsoever.

The thing was that Samuel had seen enough of the life as a small boy and through adolescence to put him off such an existence for ever. He loved his parents and life at home had always been good – but there was never any peace. From morning till late at night there was noise and bustle and never a moment just to sit and enjoy some peace and quiet. From a very early age, Samuel, Sam to all who knew him, had resolved to find gainful employment in which he could work diligently in quiet and on occasion call his time his own. And so he became a gardener.

As a youngster he had begun a small garden of his own in the back yard of the inn, round behind the sheds and the barn. His early efforts had their failures, but they were failures in the quiet, undisturbed by the clamour of others demanding attention. He was not slow to realise that among his father's customers were farmers and growers from whom he could learn just by listening, and who later, once they were aware of his hobby, would answer his questions and even come and look at his little garden. His parents encouraged him in his hobby, for, whilst they did all he could wish of them, there were times when the bar of an inn was not the best place for a small boy.

And so he grew up, quiet and well-mannered, attentive and appreciative, but determined to follow a life with plants and nature which would give him the peace and tranquility he enjoyed. With so many local contacts through the inn, he had no difficulty in finding work in one of the many small farms – it was really a market garden – and his first employer soon realised that he had a 'natural' on his hands. He learned quickly, always asking and always listening, and it was not long before he moved on to work in the gardens of a wealthy family, where he could develop his undoubted talent. As a gardener, he became a man who had both the temperament and the time to think, and as he worked with his plants he had many an earnest conversation with himself, sorting out the problems which life presented.

Working constantly to satisfy the garden-wishes of someone else was something he sometimes found irksome, and began seriously to want a post where he could plan as well as tend. His employer was well-connected in Jerusalem, and it was ironic that because of those connections he was about to lose the best gardener he had ever had. The authorities were looking to appoint someone to co-ordinate work in public gardens in the city, and Sam's name had come to their attention through the very man for whom he worked. An invitation, and then an offer, was made, and after some short negotiation Sam found himself in what he saw as the most desirable position. Not his own boss exactly, but as an expert employee with overall responsibility for gardens and cemeteries alike. For Sam, it was the job of a lifetime, and it was his at the age of thirty-eight. His delight was total.

He had been in the job now for some two years, and was held in high regard by all who saw the results of his labours. He lived now in the city, but still payed regular visits to his parents, who were justly proud of their son who had done so well, even if now and then they regretted that he had elected not to follow them into the family business. Of all his duties, there was one which gave Sam particular satisfaction, and gave his friends some amusement too. He found great peace of mind in tending the local cemetery, which to him was a place of contemplation and peace. He had long since been able to ignore the sly remarks about 'not being disturbed by the neighbours', remarks which he had at first found offensive but had soon come to dismiss them as ignorant rubbish.

As always, Passover this year had entailed much work, and the crowds in the city seemed larger than ever for some reason. The place had been a scene of great excitement, almost turmoil, ever since the Sunday before Passover, when this man, Jesus, had come riding in on a donkey, surrounded by his supporters. Some said he was a prophet, some a preacher, some others just thought him a madman. Apparently, he had said at one stage that he would rise from the dead three days after his death! Sam thought with a statement like that, he probably was a madman, but he had no time to stop and think that one out. He was far too busy to worry about cranks.

As he went about the city through the week, Sam found that the presence of this man, Jesus, was causing increasing tension as opinions formed and hardened about his preachings. Since his arrival to great acclaim, almost adulation, reaction was now setting in and there was a hard core of opposition growing by the hour. By Passover Day, Thursday, that opposition was ever more vociferous, and on the evening of the hallowed day the man had actually been arrested and put on trial. Friday had seen such a violent reaction to a man as Sam had never before experienced, except perhaps once, when he was still a small boy of seven, one day in Bethlehem.

He had often thought about the very strange happenings that day, happenings which no-one had ever explained satisfactorily, when armed men had descended on his father's inn, demanding to know of any children under two. Sam had heard that some of these babes were actually killed, and recalled the fury of the soldiers when they learned of the birth of a baby at the inn a day or so before, and of the sudden departure of both baby and parents. Sam had liked that baby, whose mother had made quite an impression with her tranquil beauty. He seemed to remember that, by some strange coincidence, he too had been called Jesus. But that was a long time ago, and all this fuss today was about a grown man who was spreading very odd teachings. After all, a lot of men had that name.

The trial, such as it was, had ended with this fellow being condemned to death by crucifixion, and the sentence had been carried out on Friday afternoon at Golgotha. Sam would have preferred to stay well clear of all this uproar, but because he would need to be ready for the burial rites he had been present on the hill when the condemned man arrived, struggling under the weight of his own cross. With him, surrounded by the screaming mob, were some of his friends and someone said even his mother was there too. Sam, so peaceful in his nature, could not bear to watch the hideous preliminaries before the cross was hoisted vertical carrying its pain-ridden burden, but, as a small group gathered round it, Sam felt compelled to look. He saw a man and a woman standing there in grief, and something about the woman caused him to draw nearer. There was something about her which struck a chord somewhere deep in his memory, but he was unsure.

He came closer, and as she turned he saw, not for the first time, her face, a face of beauty and tranquility, even at such a time. Sam paused, thunderstruck, for he recognised that face. Yes, he had seen it before, and then it had made a lasting impression on the mind of a small boy of seven! Yes, he had seen that lovely face before – in a shed behind his father's inn in Bethlehem all those years ago. The hair was grey now, and the figure slightly stooped, but Sam would have known the face anywhere, even after the passage of thirty-three years. This tragic mother was the mother of that baby, Jesus, the mother who had departed so hastily with husband and child from the inn. The bloodied figure on that cross was far removed from the baby he had once held and had enjoyed so much. His father had sometimes reminded him of his words when that little family had fled in such haste, and he recalled them again at this moment. He had said, 'I liked that baby – they called him Jesus, you know. Do you think we'll ever hear what happened to him?' He now knew the answer to his query.

Sam trembled at the memory, and withdrew from that dreadful scene to find some peace in his favourite place, among his plants. He spent the next day, the Sabbath, in silent contemplation of what he had seen, little knowing what the Sunday had in store for him. Conscientious as ever, Sam set off for the cemetery that Sunday morning, aware that 'his Jesus', as he now thought of him, had been laid in an empty, unused tomb, and that the entrance had been sealed with a great boulder. He knew, too, that the authorities had taken this prophecy about 'rising from the dead in three days' seriously, so seriously indeed that an armed guard had been mounted to forestall any possibility of cheating on the part of the man's supporters. At the time, Sam had thought that such a fuss was nothing more than that – a fuss, and about nothing. Rising from the dead indeed! Whatever next?

However, Sam's recognition of the mother on Friday had given him pause for thought. But now! The guards were gone, the boulder was rolled back, and the tomb was empty. How could that be? Sam had seen the body. There was no doubt that the man was dead, none at all. But here, at the entrance, were two men and two women who were saying that Jesus was not here, that he had risen from the dead. There was no sign that anyone had stolen the body! Indeed, the cloths which had wrapped the body were lying to one side, neatly folded and in order, just as one would have left nightclothes by the bed in the morning. Sam trembled in his wonder. He had seen his Jesus born, had seen him die. And now?